MAMMALS

gray squirrel

NATIONAL GEOGRAPHIC NATURE LIBRARY

MAMMALS

NATIONAL GEOGRAPHIC NATURE LIBRARY

by M. Barbara Brownell

Copyright © 1993 National Geographic Society
Library of Congress CIP Data: p. 60

lowland gorillas

Table of Contents

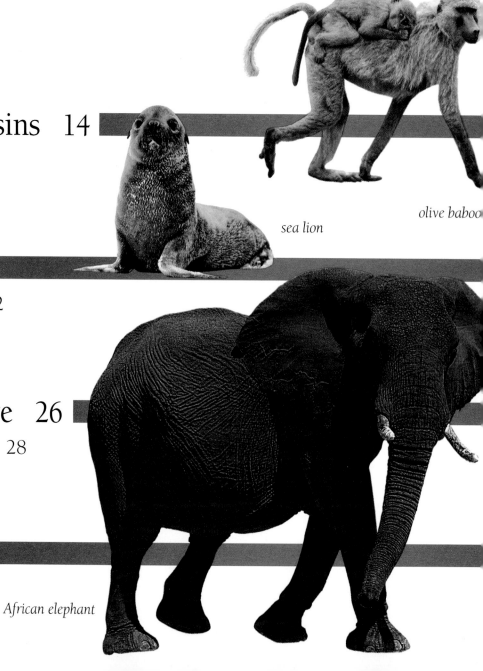

lioness with c

sea lion

olive baboo

African elephant

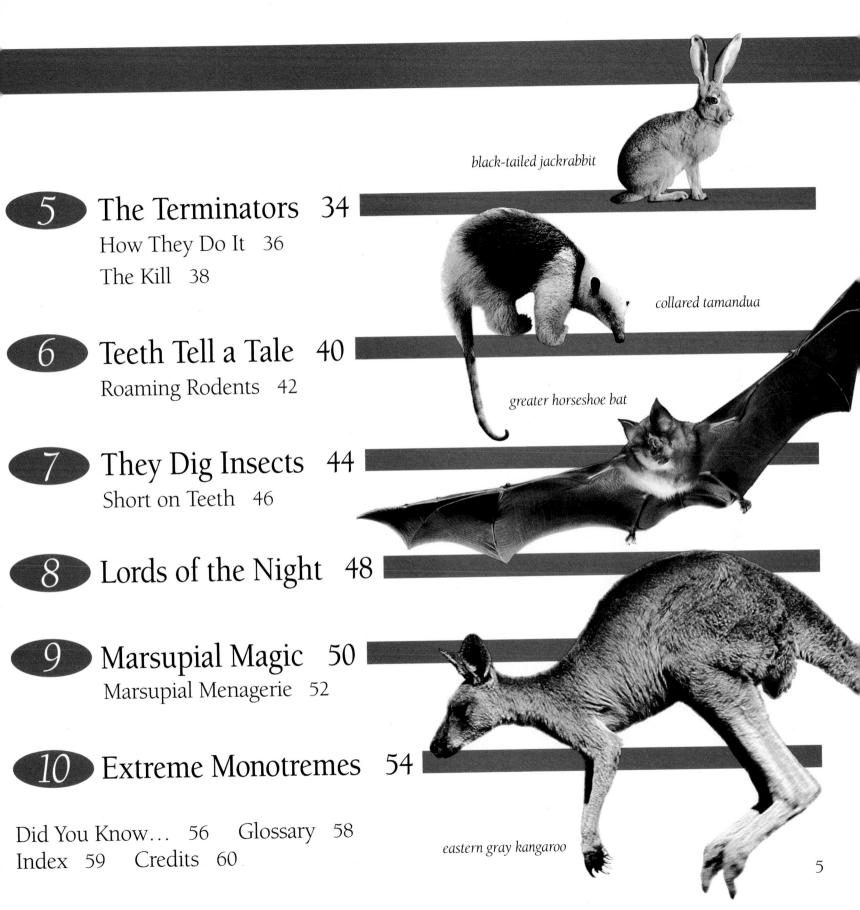

black-tailed jackrabbit

collared tamandua

greater horseshoe bat

eastern gray kangaroo

WHAT IS A MAMMAL?

Welcome to the world of mammals. Here are just a few of your relatives. On these pages you will find out about them. Altogether there are 4,200 kinds of mammals. Each one may look different, but in certain ways all of them are alike. If you ever wonder if an animal is a mammal, run through the checklist below.

All mammals are alike in these ways:

- They have HAIR.
- They are VERTEBRATES (VURT-uh-bruts).
- They BREATHE AIR.
- They are WARM-BLOODED.
- They NURSE THEIR YOUNG.

African elephant

walrus

jerboa

black-tailed jackrabbit

crested porcupine

long-eared bat

colobus
monkey

reticulated giraffe

killer whale

horse

grizzly bear

aardvark

gray
kangaroo

7

Hair, Hair, Everywhere

All mammals have hair in one form or another. Some have a lot of it, some have a little. Hair can be straight and silky soft like a cat's fur or coarse and curly like a sheep's wool. Hair is sometimes stiff, the way whiskers and eyelashes are. Or it can be as sharp as a needle. Hair protects a mammal's skin from sun and from wind. It also helps keep cold air out and hold body heat in.

NEATNESS COUNTS
Most mammals groom themselves to keep clean. They lick their hair with their rough, wet tongues. They scratch their fur with their claws or nibble it with their teeth. Mammals also groom their young and each other.

Long guard hair sheds water and protects mammals from thorns, rocks, sun, rain, and snow. Soft, short underfur helps hold in body heat.

HAIR HELPS
This family of snow monkeys only looks chilly. Thick hair helps snow monkeys, or macaques, survive in the mountains of Japan. They are the only monkeys that live where it gets very cold.

JUST HANGING AROUND
A furry dormouse has three kinds of hair—long outer hair, a thick undercoat of short hair, and a lot of twitchy whiskers. Dormice range through Europe, Asia, and Africa.

8

Whiskers are long, stiff hairs that are sensitive to touch. They help the animal feel its way, even in the dark.

THERE'S HAIR THERE
Some mammals have weird-looking hair. A porcupine has a spiky hairdo. Each sharp quill is a hair. The quills help the porcupine defend itself. An armadillo has tufts of hair hidden beneath its armor plates.

HAIR? WHERE?
Elephant seals have little hair on their bodies, and a few whiskers sprout near their noses. Instead of fur, elephant seals have a thick layer of fat called blubber that keeps them warm in icy water.

The Amazing Machines

Mammals are warm-blooded. That means their bodies stay at almost the same temperature even when temperatures around them vary. Every mammal has a backbone made up of many smaller bones called vertebrae. These bend so that the mammal can bend in various ways and in different directions. The body of every female mammal has mammary (MAM-er-ee) glands that fill with milk she feeds to her young. Milk is the first food a mammal eats, whether it is a human baby or a piglet.

MAMMAL BABIES

Some mammals, such as bears, have only one, two, or three babies at a time. Others, such as pigs, have many. Small mammals, which are prey for larger mammals, usually have a lot of babies.

A dog cannot sweat. It must pant to cool off.

You sweat one quart of water every hour when the temperature is 100° Fahrenheit.

A polar bear usually has two cubs. They are born deaf, blind, and helpless in a winter den.

WHEW!

When it is hot, a mammal can cool off to maintain its internal body temperature. A boy sweats. Sweat takes heat out of his body through openings in his skin called pores. A dog cools off by panting. When it pants, it expels hot air from its lungs.

MILK: IT'S NUMBER ONE

All winter long, polar bear cubs are nursed by their mother, who lives off her own fat. The milk a mother feeds her baby when she nurses it helps it grow fast and stay healthy. The length of time a baby nurses varies, depending on the mammal. An elephant nurses up to 4 years!

Polar bear cubs stay with their mother for two years. During that time, she feeds them, protects them, and teaches them to hunt.

backbone

BEND THAT BACKBONE!
Every mammal has a backbone. Birds and fish have backbones, too, but they lack hair and milk glands, so they cannot be mammals.

Big, Small, Short, Tall

Mammals live in many environments throughout the world. A mammal's almost unchanging body temperature lets it live in different climates. Mammals make their homes on mountains, under the ground, in deserts, on the ice, and in the water.

Dall's sheep are also known as thinhorns.

Mountain goats have horns that usually grow straight up and then curve back.

HIGH AND LOW

Each species, or kind, of mammal has adapted to survive in a certain type of home. Up high, Dall's sheep and mountain goats scale rocky cliffs. They have thick fur for warmth and rubbery hooves for gripping the rocks.

Down low in dry grasslands, prairie dogs burrow in underground tunnels.

BIG AND SMALL

Mammals come in all shapes and sizes. An African rhinoceros can weigh as much as a car. It has thick skin and two nose horns for fighting enemies. A tiny mouse might dwell in your house. It scurries away from enemies.

Prairie dogs sleep, raise their young, and find shelter underground. They live in the flat, open grasslands of the western United States.

12

ELEPHANT SEAL

UROPEAN MOLE

OUC LANGUR

HIPPOPOTAMUS

HOUSE CAT

JAGUAR

THREE-TOED SLOTH

BISON

FAMILY ALBUM

Mammals do not look or ct alike. Some are fast, others are slow. Some are entle, some fierce, some uge, and others tiny.

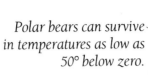
Polar bears can survive in temperatures as low as 50° below zero.

HOT AND COLD

Polar bears roam sea ice far from land in search of seals and young walruses to eat. Cold winds and icy water do not bother a polar bear. Its thick, shaggy fur works just like a blanket.

In the heat of a desert, a camel keeps its cool. It can go for several weeks without drinking water. It gets moisture from eating desert plants. Arabian camels have one hump. Bactrian (BACK-tree-un) camels have two humps.

Camels can bear temperatures above 120° Fahrenheit.

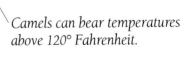

13

 Primates: Our Cousins

Human beings are primates. So are monkeys and apes. Primates can sit, stand, or walk upright, which leaves their hands free to do other jobs. They use their hands to bring food to their mouths and to pick up things. Some primates, such as apes, have large and complicated brains. Humans have the biggest brains of all primates.

GET A GRIP!
This baby primate is grabbing its mother's finger. Primates are the only mammals that can use their thumbs to grip objects.

elongated finger for digging

THE BETTER TO SEE YOU
The African bushbaby lives in trees. Its huge eyes help it hunt at night. Its flexible fingers bend to grab gnats that fly by.

AYE-AYE!
Like the bushbaby, the aye-aye is nocturnal, which means it is active at night. It digs insects out from under bark with its long, thin middle finger.

HE'S A HOWL
Adult male howler monkeys roar loudly for about 30 minutes when they wake up in the morning. They want to broadcast the location of their group and warn other monkeys to stay away.

I LOVE YOU!

An orangutan mother cuddles her baby
just as your parent hugs you.
All primate mothers care for their babies
until they can look after themselves.

*Orangutan mothers
and their young
usually stay together
for six or seven years.*

Thumbs Up!

Only a primate can touch the thumb of one hand to the fingertips of that same hand. A primate's thumb can bend to face the other fingers. Together, the thumb and fingers can make a strong grip, called a power grip, for holding things tightly. They can also make a gentle, or precision, grip. Humans use a precision grip for writing and for picking up a berry without crushing it.

The thumb of a baboon or a human rotates and can be placed flat against a finger.

HANDY HANDS

Hands of primates vary according to where they live and what they eat. Primates that live in trees have big toes for grasping branches. Pads of sensitive skin on the undersides of a primate's fingers and toes help it feel and grip.

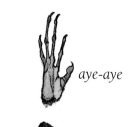 *aye-aye*

 *spider monkey*

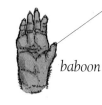 *baboon*

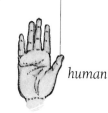 *human*

HANDS ON

A strong grip helps a baby olive baboon cling to its mother's fur. At night, the baboons use their hands to climb trees, where they can sleep in safety. There are seven species of baboons, and they live in Africa. Baboons live mainly on the ground.

16

MONKEY BUSINESS

Spider monkeys, star acrobats, can make long leaps from tree to tree. They use their hook-like hands to grip branches and swing through the treetops. A spider monkey has a strong, bending tail that grips like a hand. Such a tail is called a prehensile tail.

An area on the underside of a spider monkey's tail has no hair. The skin is very sensitive, like the skin of a human finger.

SPEEDY SWINGER

Gibbons have very long arms and strong grips. They swing hand over hand along branches, much as you go across overhead bars at a playground. Gibbons are apes. Apes are primates that lack tails.

17

Party Primates

Primates are social animals, which means they enjoy being together. Many primates live in groups. They work together and communicate with each other by making sounds and signs. And they have fun. They play tag and turn somersaults. Young primates rely on their mothers for physical and emotional support.

CHIMPANZEES IN ACTION

The sun is up! You comb your hair, eat breakfast, and say good morning. Chimps in Africa do much the same thing. They pick dirt from each other. They use grass or twigs to fish for termites. They talk by making faces, and even kiss and hold hands.

HOMEBODIES ▶

A gorilla family relaxes in its forest home. Gorillas live in groups. They protect their young and teach them to be good family members.

UH-OH

This young gorilla is learning to express itself. Like human children, young gorillas communicate by making sounds and signs. That includes making faces.

Primates groom each other to help keep themselves clean. Grooming also helps them feel close to each other.

Using tools is a characteristic of some primates. This chimp uses a stick to pull insects from a log.

② Fabulous Fins

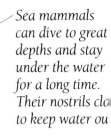

At first glance, sea mammals look more like fish than marnmals. They have smooth bodies, and they have flippers and fins instead of arms and legs. To stay warm, sea mammals depend on thick blubber instead of thick hair. Some never leave the water. To help remember that they are mammals, try this rhyme: Their blood is warm, they all have hair, and every one comes up for air.

Sea mammals can dive to great depths and stay under the water for a long time. Their nostrils clo to keep water ou

FLEXIBLE FLIPPERS ▶
A fur seal is as graceful as a ballerin in the water, but it is very clumsy on land. There are more than 30 different kinds of seals.

UP FOR AIR
A harp seal pokes its head through a breathing hole it made in the ice. Some seals use air so slowly that they can stay underwater for two hours at a time.

A MERMAID?
That is what sailors hundreds of years ago thought the manatee was. Manatees are also called sea cows. They live in warm, shallow waters and eat up to 100 pounds of sea grasses and water plants each day.

BODY BASICS
Fish and sea mammals, both super swimmers, move differently. A fish wiggles its tail fin and body from side to side. A sea mammal moves its tail up and down. Its flippers and tail fins are stronger than those of a fish.

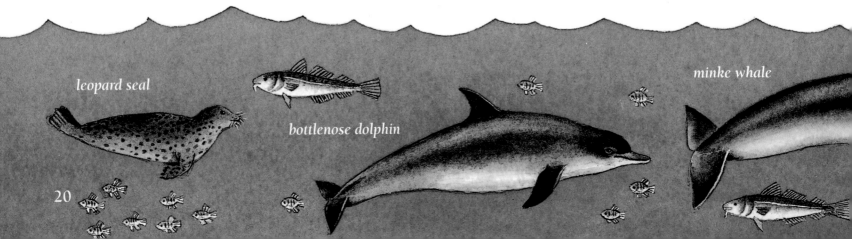

leopard seal

bottlenose dolphin

minke whale

manatee

21

Family Fun in the Sun

Some sea mammals, such as seals and walruses, are adapted for life on land as well as in the water. These are the pinnipeds (PIN-uh-pedz), or fin-footed sea mammals. Pinnipeds return to land to meet their mates and raise their young. On land, the whole family can relax in the sun.

EAR'S THE DIFFERENCE
Eared seals, such as sea lions, can bend the hind flippers forward and walk on land. Earless seals, such as leopard seals, cannot bend their hind flippers forward.

CALL OF THE WILD
"I'm the King!" a male fur seal roars to warn other males to stay away. His family may include 40 females and all their babies.

Pinnipeds have claws on their flippers. Walruses use their three middle claws to groom themselves.

HUSKY TUSKS
Walruses have huge teeth called tusks. A male walrus, or bull, uses his tusks to guard his beach. Skin up to two inches thick helps protect a walrus, and a layer of blubber up to six inches thick helps keep it warm in the icy Arctic regions where it lives.

Tusks are used as ice choppers as well as weapons.

BLOW THAT NOSE!
Elephant seals are the biggest pinnipeds. Male elephant seals use their huge noses like horns to blast out roars that warn other seals to stay away.

Only sea lions and fur seals have visible ears.

OUT IN THE COLD
Many kinds of seals live in icy water. Some seals, such as this baby sea lion, have more hair than others. Every kind of seal has a thick layer of blubber lining its skin that protects the animal from low temperatures and helps keep it warm.

Its streamlined shape helps a seal torpedo through the water.

A sea lion props itself up on its front flippers.

23

Whale of a Time

Whales never leave the water. They are almost hairless and have long, streamlined bodies. Whales can stay underwater for hours at a time. They even bear their young underwater. Sooner or later, of course, whales must surface to breathe. They range in size from small dolphins to giant blue whales, the biggest animals on earth.

IN THE SWIM
Strong front flippers help a whale steer. Powerful, flat tail fins, called flukes, move up and down. They help the whale swim fast, leap high, and even turn somersaults. Whales live in all the oceans of the world.

DOLPHIN DANCE
Bottlenose dolphins are small whales. Like all whales, they breathe through nostrils, called blowholes, on the tops of their heads. When a whale surfaces, it takes a breath.

BIG MOUTH
A killer whale, or orca, has big teeth and powerful jaws. Like all toothed whales, orcas have only one blowhole. Most toothed whales are small.

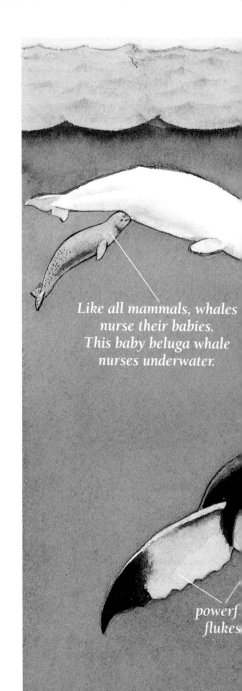

Like all mammals, whales nurse their babies. This baby beluga whale nurses underwater.

powerful flukes

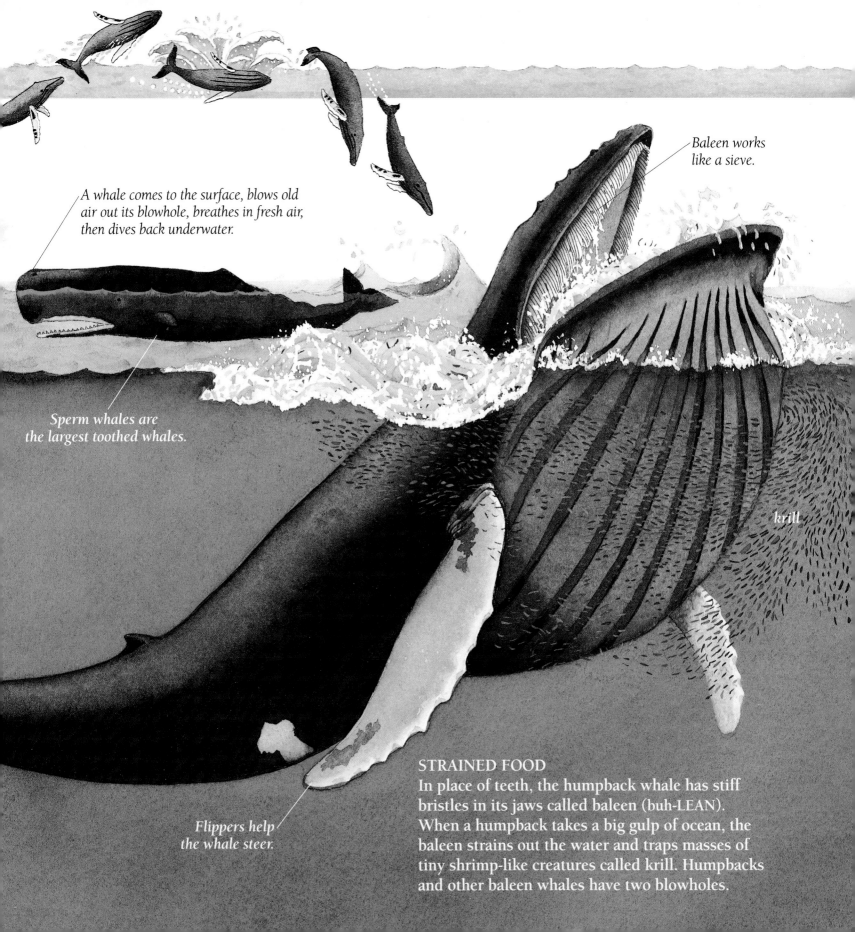

Baleen works
like a sieve.

A whale comes to the surface, blows old
air out its blowhole, breathes in fresh air,
then dives back underwater.

Sperm whales are
the largest toothed whales.

krill

Flippers help
the whale steer.

STRAINED FOOD
In place of teeth, the humpback whale has stiff
bristles in its jaws called baleen (buh-LEAN).
When a humpback takes a big gulp of ocean, the
baleen strains out the water and traps masses of
tiny shrimp-like creatures called krill. Humpbacks
and other baleen whales have two blowholes.

3 Hooves on the Move

Mammals that have hooves, such as deer, antelopes, and horses, are ungulates (UN-gya-letz). Instead of claws, ungulates have hooves—hard, curved toenails—that protect their feet. All hoofed mammals have long, strong legs and small feet. Each hoof has a particular shape that helps the animal survive where it lives.

Hoofed mammals are fast runners. They come in a wide variety of shapes and sizes.

TOUGH HOOVES
A giraffe has hooves shaped to help carry its great weight. A camel's wide hooves will not sink into desert sand. A mountain goat's split, rubbery hooves cling to rocky cliffs.

GIRAFFE

CAMEL

YIPES, STRIPES!
Zebras, like many hoofed mammals, live in herds because they offer some protection from predators. Hoofed mammals are prey for many carnivores.

EAT, LOOK, AND LISTEN
Like all hoofed mammals, the gerenuk has eyes and ears on the sides of its head so that it can look and listen for enemies as it eats. Gerenuks, which are related to gazelles, live in eastern Africa.

The gerenuk is sometimes called a giraffe-gazelle because of its long neck and feeding habits.

MOUNTAIN GOAT

ON, DASHER!

The caribou is North America's reindeer.
It has wide, flat hooves shaped like snowshoes that
help it gallop across deep snow without sinking in.

Lending Helping Hooves

Next to dogs, hoofed mammals just may be man's best friends. These are the mammals people have domesticated, or tamed, so that we can use their milk, meat, or wool. We also use them for transportation. Most hoofed mammals are plant-eaters. Giraffes eat leaves. Cows eat grass. Pigs eat almost anything.

A sheep wears about eight pounds of wool. Most sheep are sheared once a year, in the spring.

HAVE YOU ANY WOOL?
Yes, sir! The wool of these sheep will be sheared, or clipped off, then spun into yarn for clothes. The haircut doesn't hurt. The wool grows back in a few months and will be snipped off again. People domesticated sheep 10,000 years ago.

THIS LITTLE PIGGY...
will soon grow fat. Farmers feed pigs corn and other grains to make their meat, called pork, tender and tasty. Wild pigs eat roots, nuts, and other plants. They seldom grow fat.

ORN BIG

baby moose is born ready to travel.
a few days, it can run faster than
man. Most hoofed mammals travel all
e time, and their young must keep up.

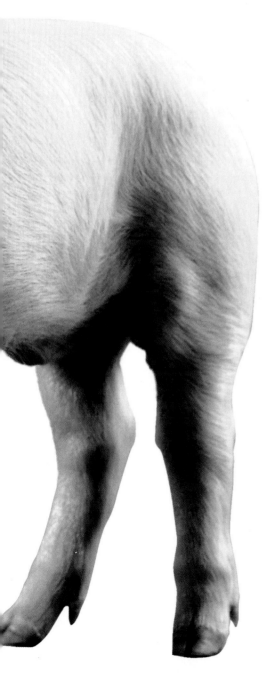

A giraffe uses its tough, 18-inch-long tongue to strip leaves off branches.

BROWSING AROUND

A giraffe reaches up high to eat
leaves. Giraffes are browsers,
mammals that eat
the shoots and leaves
of trees and shrubs.
A cow or a sheep
bends down to nibble
grass. Mammals that
eat grasses are
known as grazers.

29

Head Dressing

Horns or antlers? They are different. Horns grow out of the skin as fingernails do, and never stop growing. Goats, antelopes, and cattle have horns. Antlers are bones that grow each year, then fall off. Male deer have antlers. Animals use horns and antlers for fighting.

BEST DRESSED DEER

In the spring, a velvety coat covers the new antlers of a male mule deer, or buck. Soon the velvet rubs off, revealing hard, shiny antlers. Deer live on every continent except Antarctica.

GROWTH RINGS

As a male bighorn sheep, or ram, ages, its horns continue to grow, curving forward and upward. Young males and female bighorns, or ewes, have short horns.

A male European red deer, called a stag, roars to tell other males to stay away. A male deer uses its sharp antlers to defend its territory from other males.

BIG BASH!

Male Barbary sheep from northern Africa butt heads to prove which ram is stronger. These sheep have manes on their throats and chests. They look more like goats than sheep.

DON'T BOTHER ME
An African buffalo only looks easygoing.
Enemies find out that his horns
are as sharp as pitchforks.

Horns grow across the
male's head and protect
it like a helmet.

An African
buffalo may
weigh as much
as 2,000
pounds. It is
one of the most
dangerous
animals in
Africa.

4 Power Trunks

Elephants are the biggest land animals. Their tusks are the world's biggest teeth, and their trunks are the biggest noses. A trunk has 100,000 muscles. It can pull a tree out of the ground, and it can pick up a feather. Family members hug with it. A mother lifts her baby with it. Its trunk helps an elephant sniff food, water, and enemies.

HUT, TWO! ▶

It's an elephant parade. Members of a herd travel in single file. All day they look for water and grass. They wave their ears like fans to cool themselves. An elephant may weigh 14,000 pounds, but it walks very quietly because its feet are padded.

NOSE TO NOSE

A mother elephant uses her trunk to pat her baby and to shade it from the sun. The calf will take a nap standing up.

African elephant

WHICH IS WHICH?

An elephant from Africa has huge ears, the size of a man. They are shaped like the continent of Africa. Its trunk has two feelers, called fingers, for picking up food. An Asian elephant has smaller ears and a rounded back. Its trunk has only one finger.

Asian elephant

32

ELEPHANT HUG
Wrapping their trunks together helps elephants feel close.

TRUNK AND TREAT!
All day an elephant pulls leaves and bark off trees with its trunk and pops them into its mouth.

SUPER STRAWS
A thirsty elephant can suck two gallons of water into its trunk at once. It squirts the water into its mouth a trunkful at a time.

5 The Terminators

They are strong. They are fast. They are the predators. Predators kill and eat other animals, called prey. Wolves, cats, badgers, and bears are predators. All are expert hunters. Predators have sharp claws for grabbing and sharp teeth for killing and for tearing meat. They see, hear, and smell well.

BLACK BEAR (NORTH AMERICA)

EYES SPY
The eyes of a cat are perfect for hunting at night. In daytime, the pupils close to slits. At night, the pupils open and let in any light.

BEAR FACTS
Bears live in North and South America, Europe, and Asia. They use their claws to dig, climb, and kill. Unlike most predators, bears eat berries, nuts, and fish as well as meat.

Tigers, which live in Asia, are the largest cats in the world. They have powerful jaws that help them capture, kill, and carry prey.

OPEN WIDE! ▶
A mighty roar reveals the rough tongue and four big canine teeth of an African lion. Predators that have these four sharp, slicing teeth are members of the group of mammals called carnivores (CAR-nuh-vorz).

A Bengal tiger's sharp, curved claws snap out to grab prey. Like all cats except the cheetah, the tiger can retract—or pull in—its claws when walking. That way the claws stay sharp.

LET THE HUNT BEGIN
A gray wolf howls to gather members of his group, called a pack. Wolves in Europe, Asia, and North America hunt together to bring down deer, moose, caribou, and other prey.

canine teeth

35

How They Do It

Some predators hunt together. Some hunt alone. Wild dogs in Africa hunt animals bigger than they are, such as buffalo and zebras. A pack of dogs must work together to catch big prey. Then the dogs share the meal. Cats usually hunt alone. They chase quick creatures smaller than themselves. First, a cat creeps closer to its prey, then it pounces. A mouse would make a meal for a house cat.

FAST FOOD

A Canada lynx chases a snowshoe hare, its favorite food. A lynx is a wild cat. It stalks its prey. Very quietly, it creeps closer and closer. Then, whoosh! It bursts forward and runs its prey down.

EASY TO PLEASE

Like wild dogs, spotted hyenas in Afri hunt together in packs to bring down large prey. Hyenas will eat almost anything, including animals that have died and the leftovers of other predat

A SINGLE STRIKE

That is all it takes for a mongoose to catch a snake. This weasel-like mongoose lives in India. Its jaws clamp onto the snake's head and crush it before the snake can strike back. Mongooses also eat insects, rodents, birds, and plants.

PACK ATTACK

A zebra kicks and bites at a pack of wild dogs on a plain in Africa. It will probably lose the fight. Wild dogs chase large prey until it is tired. Then they circle it and pull it down.

The Kill

Splash! Snort! Snarl! A predator may catch prey on land, underground, in the water, or in midair. Predators have teeth shaped for snatching, cutting, and tearing meat. A predator is usually quiet as it approaches its prey. It runs, crouches, and leaps. It bites, swats, or grabs the prey, and holds it tight. After eating, a predator often naps.

DIGGING IN ▶
A North American badger like this one finds some of its best meals underground. It uses its sharp claws to dig up mice and insects. A European badger digs for worms. It slurps them up like spaghetti.

LEADER OF THE PACK
A gray wolf in Minnesota guards a deer that its pack has just killed. This wolf is probably the leader. Leaders eat from the kill first. Less important wolves get the leftovers.

MEAL IN A MINUTE

This lucky brown bear in Alaska just opens its mouth, and in pops a salmon. Usually, the bear has to do a belly flop into the river and pin down the fish with its paw.

Foxes live throughout the world. They are clever at finding food and will eat rodents, eggs, and fruit.

The thick, bushy tail of a fox is sometimes called a brush.

GOTCHA!

A pheasant is a tasty meal for a red fox. The fox creeps up and waits. When the bird takes off, the fox springs into the air and grabs it. To catch a mouse, the fox leaps up and pounces with its front feet.

39

6 Teeth Tell a Tale

Rabbits, hares, and pikas belong to a group of mammals called lagomorphs (LAG-uh-morfs). Their top teeth are shaped like chisels and never stop growing. All day lagomorphs nip and chew grasses and bark. This keeps their teeth from growing too long. Lagomorphs have big ears and feet—and noses that wiggle.

THERE'S A HARE
A baby hare huddles quietly. Only its nose twitches. Its coat blends with the grass, so predators cannot see it.

The long ears of a hare are often tipped with black.

A jackrabbit is about 19 inches long, plus a 4-inch tail.

HEADS UP!
If a rabbit senses trouble, it perks up its ears to listen. It freezes. If danger nears, the rabbit runs for cover. Rabbits are prey for many other mammals. To make sure that some of their babies escape predators and grow up, rabbits have a lot of young.

Eyes on the side of its head allow a lagomorph to watch for predators as it eats.

LAGOMORPH LOOKS
Hares and rabbits are close relatives, and both live all over the world. Hares and rabbits look alike. Even their names are confusing. A jackrabbit is really a hare. Hares are usually bigger than rabbits, and their ears and furry hind feet are longer.

NO TIME OUT
A pika hardly ever rests.
All day long it scurries through
its mountain home gathering
food. If danger nears, the pika
barks to warn its family. Pikas
are just 6 to 10 inches long.

HOP TO IT!
An arctic hare hurries
into action when
danger is close. Strong
legs help it sprint faster
than most other
mammals. Arctic hares
live in Canada. When
snow covers the
ground, their fur is
white to match their
environment.

SNACK-PACKING PIKA
Pikas never seem to get enough
grasses, twigs, and mosses to eat.
In warm weather, they stock up
on extra food and store it to eat
during the winter.

Roaming Rodents

Nearly half of all the different kinds of mammals on earth are rodents. Among them are squirrels, mice, and gerbils. Rodents live in an assortment of environments almost everywhere on earth. Like lagomorphs, rodents have long, chisel-shaped teeth and eat constantly to keep them short. Some rodents have cheek pouches.

GRAY SQUIRREL (NORTH AMERICA)

Webbed back feet serve as swim fins, pushing a beaver through the water.

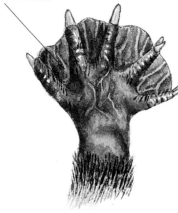

NUTS!
Gnawing keeps this squirrel's teeth short. Most rodents hold their food between their front paws as they eat.

TINY BUT TOUGH
A hard orange covering called keratin covers a rodent's teeth. It strengthens the teeth for all the gnawing and grinding a rodent does.

LEAVE IT TO A BEAVER
All day long a beaver chews bark. It may gnaw a tree down and use the branches to build a dam or a lodge. On land, a beaver waddles. In water, it swims fast and well. Beavers live in rivers, lakes, and streams in North America and parts of Europe and Asia.

A tail longer than its body helps the kangaroo rat steer and keep its balance.

CHEEK STORAGE
Loading up for a long winter, a chipmunk stuffs acorns into pouches in its cheeks. It stores the nuts for snacking when food is hard to find.

BERRY GOOD
A house mouse stretches up
to nibble a plump blackberry.
It may carry bits of berry home
in its cheeks.

ROVING RAT
Long whiskers help a little
vesper rat in Central America
feel its way to find fruit.
Vesper rats hunt at night.
Other rats eat fish, garbage,
and anything else they
can find.

*A beaver's wide tail acts as
a rudder. The beaver uses it
to steer up or down, right or
left. It slaps the water with its
tail to warn other beavers
when danger threatens.*

*Kangaroo rats
get moisture
from the plants,
insects, and
seeds they eat.*

BOING!
This little bouncer is a kangaroo rat.
It hops across the desert like a kangaroo.
Its big hind feet keep it from sinking into
the sand. Kangaroo rats live in desert and
dry areas of North America.

7 They Dig Insects

A tree trunk full of bugs would be a feast for shrews, moles, and hedgehogs. These mammals are called insectivores (in-SEK-tuh-vorz) because they eat mainly insects. Insectivores have bad eyesight and long, sensitive snouts that help them find prey. Moles munch worms, hedgehogs hunt ants, and solenodons snack on beetles. Some insectivores also eat snakes and lizards.

WHAT'S UP? ▶
A European mole pops out of a tunnel it has dug. Moles are nearly blind, but they do not nee[d] to see. Underground, where they live, their sensitive snouts and whiskers help them get around.

shaped the same at both ends

ON GUARD!
Insects beware of the elephant shrew's long, flexible snout. It pokes under leaves for food. The prickly spines of a hedgehog help protect it from predators while it eats.

ELEPHANT SHREW (AFRICA)

HEDGEHOG (EUROPE)

MIGHTY MOLE
A mole digs like a power shovel. Its sharp claws push dirt away, while its powerful body shoves forward. It can move backward easily, too, thanks to a body pointed at both ends.

long snout for probi[ng] for insects

NOSE ALERT
The foot-long solenodon, one of the largest insectivores, lives on two islands in the West Indies. It bites its prey, injecting poisonous saliva. Solenodons also eat birds, lizards, and snake[s]

Short on Teeth

Think about these word parts. "E" means "missing," "dent" means "tooth," and "ate" means "creature." Together the parts spell "edentate" (e-DEN-tate). An edentate has few teeth or no teeth. Edentates, which include armadillos and anteaters, usually hunt at night. They have long snouts for sniffing prey, sharp claws for breaking into anthills and termite mounds, and sticky tongues for slurping up meals.

PANGOLINS ON A ROLL

This mother and baby pangolin are about to rip apart an ant nest with their sharp claws. A pangolin can close its nostrils, eyes, and ears so that biting insects cannot crawl in. Pangolins live in Africa and Asia.

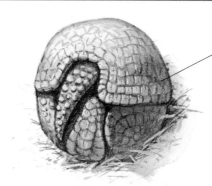

An armadillo rolls up into a tight ball.

overlapping pieces of thick skin for protection

GETTING THE GRUB

When a log is jam-packed with insects called grubs, an armadillo may feast there all day long. Armadillos are found in the southern United States and South America. A shell made of bony plates, like armor, covers the armadillo. If an enemy approaches, the armadillo curls into a hard little ball.

The tamandua (tuh-MAN-duh-wuh) is an anteater about the size of a raccoon.

KNOCK, KNOCK
An anteater sniffs out an anthill or a termite mound like this one, digs a hole in it, then flicks in its tongue. Gluey saliva covers the tongue so that insects stick to it. Anteaters range from South America into Mexico.

*sensitive snout
for locating prey*

*long, worm-like tongue
for reaching prey*

*strong claws for digging
and for defense*

SMALL AND SOFT
This squirrel-size silky anteater in Costa Rica got its name from its soft fur. It lives in South American rain forests, and spends almost all of its time in trees.

8 Lords of the Night

Bats are the only mammals that can fly. They fly as well as birds—but bats have fur instead of feathers. Their wings are covered with smooth, leathery skin. A bat flaps its strong wings to swoop, glide, and somersault. There are about a thousand kinds of bats, and they are found all over the world. Most eat insects, many eat fruit, and a few eat small vertebrates.

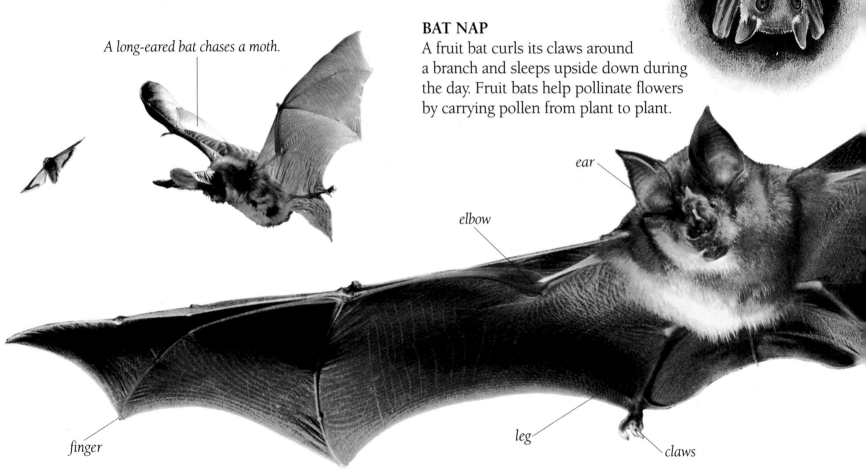

A long-eared bat chases a moth.

BAT NAP
A fruit bat curls its claws around a branch and sleeps upside down during the day. Fruit bats help pollinate flowers by carrying pollen from plant to plant.

ear

elbow

finger

leg

claws

SWOOP AND SCOOP
Bats feed mainly at night. They use their ears instead of their eyes to find their way, avoid obstacles, and locate prey. When flying, a bat makes squeaking sounds. The squeaks bounce off an insect. The bat hears the echo and can determine where the insect is. This method of locating prey by listening to an echo is called echolocation (ek-oh-low-KAY-shun). A single bat can gobble up 500 to 1,000 mosquitoes in an hour.

The skin of a bat's wings connects its legs, arms, fingers, and hook-like thumbs.

thumb

finger

finger

VAMPIRE BAT

VESPER BAT

LEAF-NOSED BAT

FRUIT BAT

BAT GALLERY

A bat uses its head to find food. The eyes, nose, and ears of each type of bat help it locate the food it prefers. A few kinds of bats are vampires, which drink blood. Their razor-sharp front teeth make tiny cuts in the skin of their prey. Fruit bats use their large eyes and long snouts to look and sniff for fruit.

NOT A BAT, NOT A BIRD

few mammals, such as the colugo and the
ing squirrel, can glide. Strong skin connects
e colugo's fingers, arms, legs, toes, and tail.
he colugo, found only in Southeast Asia, climbs
tree, spreads its skin, sails to another tree,
imbs up it, and glides down again.

9 Marsupial Magic

Female marsupials (mar-SOO-pea-ulz) have pouches on their bellies and give birth to tiny, underdeveloped babies. A newborn marsupial crawls into its mother's pouch and nurses until it can survive outside. Most marsupials, such as kangaroos, live in Australia. Elsewhere, most mammals are placental mammals, which means the young live inside their mother for a longer time and are born more developed.

PIGGYBACK OPOSSUMS
The opossum is the only marsupial in North America. Opossums live only two years, but have as many as 20 young at a time. At birth, the bee-size babies are blind and hairless. They climb into their mother's pouch and stay there about two months. After that, they cling to her back.

HOME SWEET HOME
For eight months, its mother's pouch is home to a young kangaroo, or joey. To enter, it puts its forepaws on the pouch, dives in, and turns a somersault. Out pops its head.

Its long tail helps the tree kangaroo balance.

CLIMBING KANGA
Climbing trees is the specialty of the colorful tree kangaroo. It grabs branches with its long forelegs and sharp claws, but it is awkward on the ground. Below, a gray kangaroo joey peeps from its mother's pouch. There are more than 50 different kinds of kangaroos.

Its muscular tail is used as a prop when the animal rests.

Even when carrying her baby, this mother kangaroo can spring six feet into the air.

BIG RED POGO STICK
A red kangaroo can jump 6 feet into the air and cover 25 feet in a single bound. Its huge feet work like springs. Red kangaroos are the largest of all marsupials. They are taller than most people and weigh more than 150 pounds.

51

Marsupial Menagerie

Like other mammals, marsupials vary in size and shape, live in many different environments, and eat various foods. Compared to the red kangaroo, most marsupials are small. All have sharp senses of smell and hearing. They are active at dawn and dusk. Some marsupials eat insects or nectar. Only a few eat meat.

NO BEAR THERE ▶
Koalas may look like bears, but they are
Koalas are marsupials. All day long, koa
climb and doze in treetops. They seldor
come down. Koalas are picky eaters.
They eat mostly eucalyptus leaves.

MINI MARSUPIAL
A sip of nectar fills up a little pygmy possum. Possums, better climbers than the American opossum, have longer, more flexible fingers.

A two-inch-long little pygmy possum has a tail as long as its entire body.

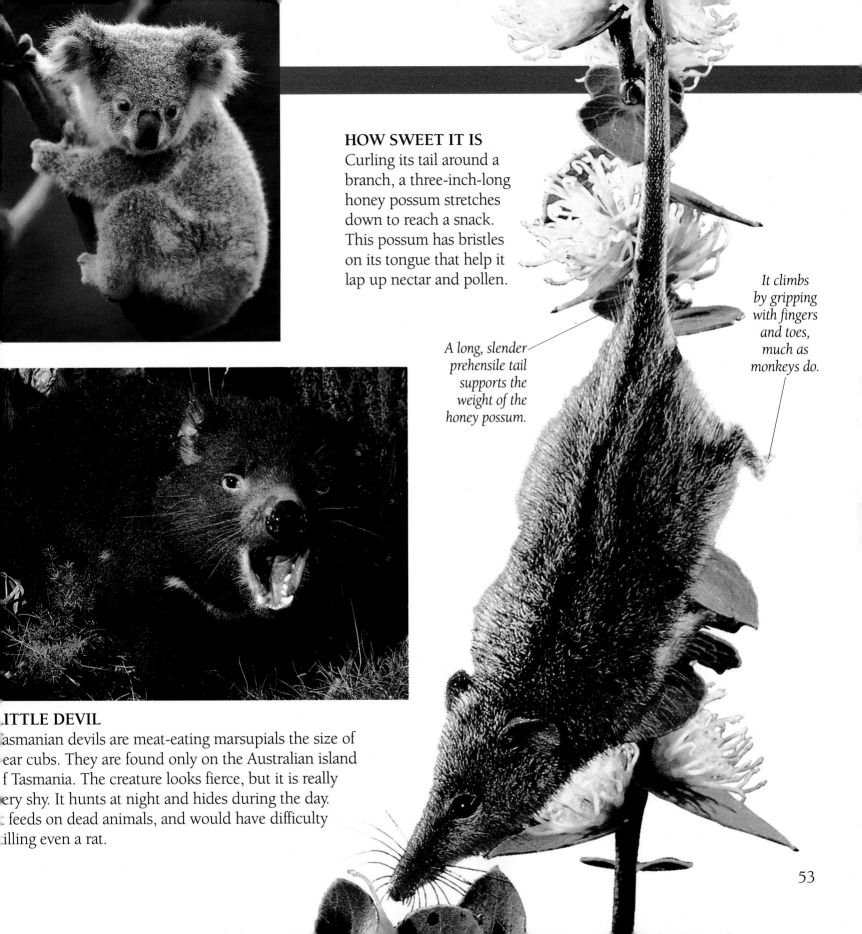

HOW SWEET IT IS
Curling its tail around a branch, a three-inch-long honey possum stretches down to reach a snack. This possum has bristles on its tongue that help it lap up nectar and pollen.

A long, slender prehensile tail supports the weight of the honey possum.

It climbs by gripping with fingers and toes, much as monkeys do.

LITTLE DEVIL
Tasmanian devils are meat-eating marsupials the size of bear cubs. They are found only on the Australian island of Tasmania. The creature looks fierce, but it is really very shy. It hunts at night and hides during the day. It feeds on dead animals, and would have difficulty killing even a rat.

53

Extreme Monotremes

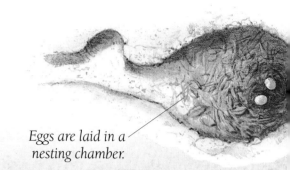

few mammals lay eggs. Egg-laying mammals are called monotremes (MON-uh-treemz). There are only two types of monotremes—the platypus and the echidna (ih-KID-nuh). They live in or near Australia. Monotreme eggs are soft and have a rubbery shell. The young hatch in about ten days.

Eggs are laid in a nesting chamber.

MIXED-UP MAMMAL

A platypus is the size of a small cat. It lives in the water and in burrows it digs in riverbanks. The platypus sweeps its sensitive bill from side to side two or three times every second to locate small animals to eat on the river bottom.

duck-like bill

webbed feet

CUDDLE UP

The female platypus lays eggs the size of grapes. She warms them between her stomach and her tail until they hatch. Her milk seeps from tiny pores on her stomach and sticks to her fur. When the babies hatch, they lap up the milk with their soft bills.

STRANGE BUT TRUE

The foot-long echidna has spines like a porcupine's, a snout like an anteater's, and a pouch like a kangaroo's. A mother echidna lays a single egg into her pouch.

beaver-like tail

LOOKING SHARP

When an echidna is frightened, it burrows rapidly into the ground. Predators get a sharp surprise. Echidnas are also called spiny anteaters.

The adult male platypus has a spur that fills with venom on the underside of each hind leg.

An echidna uses its long, sticky tongue to zap termites and ants.

55

Did You Know...

1 **THAT** the aardvark is one of a kind? It is not closely related to any other mammal. Aardvarks live in the forests and grasslands of Africa. They are about six feet long from nose to tail. Aardvarks use their sharp claws to burrow into termite mounds and scarf up the insects with their long tongues.

2 **THAT** meerkats take turns guarding their burrows? They stand at the entrance and watch for eagles and hawks. Meerkats are also called suricates. They live in packs and eat insects and larvae. A meerkat is a squirrel-size kind of mongoose that lives only in southern Africa. ▶

3 **THAT** a klipspringer can land in an area smaller than a cup? Klipspringers are little antelopes that live in steep, rocky areas of Africa. They have hooves that work like rubber suction cups so that they can leap from ledge to ledge. Only male klipspringers have horns.

4 **THAT** sloths are the slowest mammals in the world? Sloths live in trees in the rain forests of Central and South America. It is so wet, and sloths move so slowly, that algae grow in their fur, tinting it green.

5 **THAT** the capybara is the world's largest rodent? Capybaras, found only in South America, are about four feet long. They spend much of their time in the water, where they eat aquatic plants. Like all rodents, capybaras must chew constantly because their front teeth never stop growing.

Glossary

ALGAE Simple forms of plant life, found mostly in water.

CARNIVORE Any member of the large group of mammals that have four big canine teeth for slicing and tearing meat. The word "carnivore" is also used generally to describe any animal that eats flesh.

CHARACTERISTIC A quality or thing that identifies an animal or makes it different from other kinds of animals.

DOMESTICATED Tamed by man to provide things such as wool, meat, cheese, and leather that people want or need.

ENVIRONMENT The place in which an animal lives—its surroundings, including air, land, and water.

FLEXIBLE Elastic, able to bend.

GAZELLE A medium-size antelope that grows ringed horns. There are about 14 kinds of gazelles.

KERATIN A tough, hard material made up of fibers that forms the outer layer of hair, nails, horns, and hooves. Keratin also covers and protects the teeth of rodents.

MAMMARY GLANDS Structures in a female mammal's body that produce milk she feeds her young.

PLACENTAL MAMMAL A mammal that gives birth to living young that are developed enough to survive outside their mother's body as soon as they are born.

POLLINATE To place pollen in a flower so that it can produce fruit and flowers.

PORE A tiny opening in the skin of an animal that fluid ca pass through.

PREDATOR An animal that hunts and kills other animals for food.

PREHENSILE Able to seize or grasp, especially by wrapping around.

PREY An animal that is hunted by other animals for food.

SNOUT The long, projecting nose of some animals.

SPECIES A group of animals of the same kind that can produce young like themselves.

SPUR A stiff, sharp spine.

STREAMLINED Having a smooth or flowing shape.

UNDERDEVELOPED Not normally developed or not developed enough to survive on its own.

VENOM A poisonous substance that is formed and transmitted by some animals, such as snakes and bees, usually by biting or stinging.

VERTEBRA One of the bony segments that make up the backbone, or spine.

VERTEBRATE An animal—fish, amphibian, reptile, bird, or mammal—with a backbone.

WARM-BLOODED Able to keep a constant body temperature even when the temperature of the surroundings var

COVER: Mandrills, largest of all monkeys, live in western Africa. Only the adult males display spectacular colors.

Printed and bound by R.R. Donnelley & Sons Company, Willard, Ohio. Color separations by Phototype Color Graphics, Pennsauken, New Jersey. Case cover printed by Southeastern Color Graphics, Johnson City, Tennessee.

ringtail possum

Credits

Published by
The National Geographic Society
Gilbert M. Grosvenor, *President
and Chairman of the Board*
Michela A. English,
Senior Vice President

Prepared by
The Book Division
William R. Gray, *Vice President and Director*
Margery G. Dunn, Charles Kogod, *Assistant Directors*

Staff for this book
Toni Eugene, *Project Editor and Text Editor*
Sharon Davis Thorpe, *Art Director*
John G. Agnone, *Illustrations Editor*
Rebecca Lescaze, *Researcher*
Jane H. Buxton, *Contributing Editor*
Marianne R. Koszorus, Cinda Rose, *Contributing Art Directors*
Heather Guwang, *Production Project Manager*
H. Robert Morrison, *Production*
Artemis S. Lampathakis, *Illustrations Assistant*
Karen F. Edwards, *Design Assistant*
Sandra F. Lotterman, Teresita Cóquia Sison, Marilyn J. Williams,
Staff Assistants
Elisabeth MacRae-Bobynskyj, *Indexer*

Manufacturing and Quality Management
George V. White, *Director;* John T. Dunn, *Associate Director;*
Vincent P. Ryan, *Manager;* and R. Gary Colbert

Acknowledgments

We are grateful for the assistance of James M. Dietz, University of Maryland; Hugh J. Lavery, Australian Environment International Party, Ltd.; Merlin Tuttle, Bat Conservation International, *Scientific Consultants.* We also thank Edward Leber for his ideas and suggestions.

Illustrations Credits

Front Matter: COVER Art Wolfe. 1 Richard Packwood/OXFORD SCIENTIFIC FILMS. 2-3 James Bal◄ 4 (top to bottom), Norman Myers/BRUCE COLEMAN INC; Richard Coomber/PLANET EARTH PICTU Kevin Schafer & Martha Hill/ALLSTOCK; Jen & Des Bartlett. 5 (top to bottom), François Gohier; Michael Fogden/DRK PHOTO; Stephen Dalton/OXFORD SCIENTIFIC FILMS; Jean-Paul Ferrero/JAC◄ 6 (art, left), Robert Cremins. 6-7 (art), Tony Chen. 8, Michio Hoshino/ALLSTOCK. 8-9 (all art) Rob◄ Cremins. 8-9 (center), Owen Newman/NATURE PHOTOGRAPHERS LTD. 9 (bottom), Art Wolfe. 10◄ 11 (art), Robert Cremins. 10 (right), Thomas Houland/GRANT HEILMAN. 10-11 (center), Wayne Lynch/DRK PHOTO. 12 and 13 (art), Robert Cremins. 13 (left, top to bottom), James D. Watt/PLAN▮ EARTH PICTURES; Leonard Lee Rue III/RUE ENTERPRISES; Vince Streano/ALLSTOCK; Frans Lanting/MINDEN PICTURES. 13 (center, top to bottom), John Livzey/ALLSTOCK; Michael and Patri▮ Fogden; Michael and Patricia Fogden; Art Wolfe.
Primates: 14 (art), Robert Cremins. 14 (left), Stephen Dalton/NHPA. 14 (top right), Charles Gupton/ALLSTOCK. 14 (bottom right), Kevin Schafer. 14-15 Tom McHugh/ALLSTOCK. 16 (art), R◄ Cremins. 16 (bottom), Richard Coomber/PLANET EARTH PICTURES. 17 (art, left and right) Tony C▮ 17 (center), Robert Cremins. 18 (art), Robert Cremins. 18 Steve Turner/OXFORD SCIENTIFIC FILM▮ 18-19 Bob Campbell.
Sea Mammals: 20 (art), Robert Cremins. 20 (left), Stephen J. Krasemann/ALLSTOCK. 20 (right), M◄ Timothy O'Keefe. 20-21 (art), Tony Chen. 20-21 (top), Anthony Bannister/NHPA. 22-23 (all art), Robert Cremins. 22 (center), Erwin & Peggy Bauer/BRUCE COLEMAN INC. 22 (bottom), Leonard L▮ Rue III/RUE ENTERPRISES. 22-23 Kevin Schafer & Martha Hill/ALLSTOCK. 24-25 (all art), Tony Ch▮ 24 (top), Stephen J. Krasemann/DRK PHOTO. 24 (bottom), Frans Lanting/MINDEN PICTURES. 26-◄ (art), Robert Cremins.
Hoofed Mammals: 26 (top and bottom), Art Wolfe. 26 (right, top to bottom), ANIMALS ANIMALS/Leonard Lee Rue III; ANIMALS ANIMALS/Adrienne T. Gibson; ANIMALS ANIMALS/Ed W◄ 26-27 (bottom), Jim Brandenburg/MINDEN PICTURES. 28 & 29 (art), Robert Cremins. 28 Art Wolfe/ALLSTOCK. 28-29 Larry Lefever/GRANT HEILMAN. 29 Art Wolfe. 30 (art), Robert Cremins. 30 (top left), Art Wolfe. 30 (bottom left), Manfred Danegger/PETER ARNOLD, INC. 30 (right), Fran▮ Lanting/MINDEN PICTURES. 30-31 Michael and Patricia Fogden.
Elephants: 32 (art), Robert Cremins. 32 Martyn Colbeck/OXFORD SCIENTIFIC FILMS. 32-33 Jen a▮ Des Bartlett. 33 (right, top to bottom), Robert Caputo; Robert Caputo; Leonard Lee Rue III/RUE ENTERPRISES.
Carnivores: 34 (art), Robert Cremins. 34 (top left), Alan and Sandy Carey. 34 (center), Mike Birkhead/OXFORD SCIENTIFIC FILMS. 34 (right), London Scientific Films/OSF. 34 (bottom left), Je▮ Ferrara. 34-35 Boyd Norton. 36 (art), Robert Cremins. 36-37 Leonard Lee Rue III/RUE ENTERPRIS▮ 36 (left), Belinda Wright/DRK PHOTO. 37 (art), Tony Chen. 38-39 Art Wolfe. 39 (art, top), Tony C▮ 39 (art, bottom), Robert Cremins. 39 (right), John Shaw/NHPA.
Lagomorphs and Rodents: 40 (art), Robert Cremins. 40 (left), G.I. Bernard/OXFORD SCIENTIFIC FILMS. 40 (bottom), François Gohier. 40-41 Stephen J. Krasemann/DRK PHOTO. 41 (art), Tony C▮ 41 (right), Art Wolfe. 42 (art, left) Robert Cremins. 42 (art, right) and 42-43 (art), Tony Chen. 42 ◄ Stephen Dalton/NHPA. 42 (center), ANIMALS ANIMALS/Breck P. Kent. 42-43 (bottom), Tom McHugh/ALLSTOCK. 43 (top), Michael & Patricia Fogden. 43 (right), Rodger Jackman/OXFORD SCIENTIFIC FILMS.
Insectivores and Edentates: 44 (art, top) Robert Cremins. 44 (art, bottom), Tony Chen. 44 (top), Anthony Bannister/NHPA. 44 (bottom), A. Gandolfi/JACANA. 44 (right), Philippe Varin/JACANA. 45 Michel Denis-Huot/JACANA. 46 and 47 (art), Robert Cremins. 46 (left), Nick Gordon/SURVIVAl ANGLIA. 46 (right), Jeff Foott. 46-47 Jany Sauvanet/NHPA. 47 Michael & Patricia Fogden.
Bats: 48 (art), Robert Cremins. 48 Stephen Dalton/NHPA. 48-49 Stephen Dalton/OXFORD SCIENTI▮ FILMS. 49 (art), Tony Chen. 49 (top left), Michael & Patricia Fogden. 49 (top right), Press-Tige Pictures/OXFORD SCIENTIFIC FILMS. 49 (bottom left), Merlin D. Tuttle/ALLSTOCK. 49 (bottom rig▮ Art Wolfe. 50 & 51 (art), Robert Cremins.
Marsupials: 50 (top left), Richard S. Diego. 50 (bottom left), Wayne Lynch/DRK PHOTO. 50-51 C▮ Andrew Henley/BIOFOTOS. 51 Bill Bachman/ALLSTOCK. 52 (art), Robert Cremins. 52 C. Andrew Henley/BIOFOTOS. 53 (top left), Art Wolfe/ALLSTOCK. 53 (bottom left), Dave Watts/JACANA. 53 (right), Babs & Bert Wells/OXFORD SCIENTIFIC FILMS.
Monotremes: 54-55 (art), Tony Chen. 54 (art, top) and 55 (art, all), Robert Cremins. 55 (center), Jean-Paul Ferrero/Auscape International 55 (lower), Kathie Atkinson/OXFORD SCIENTIFIC FILMS.
Back Matter: 56 (art), and 57 (art, bottom), Robert Cremins. 56 Tom McHugh/ALLSTOCK. 57 (art, top), Tony Chen. 57 David McDonald/OXFORD SCIENTIFIC FILMS. 60 Lloyd Nielsen/OXFORD SCIENTIFIC FILMS.

Library of Congress CIP Data
Brownell, M. Barbara.
    Mammals / by M. Barbara Brownell.
        p.   cm. — (National Geographic nature library)
    Includes index.
    Summary: Defines what mammals are and examines the characteristics and behavior of various primates, sea mammals▮ ungulates, rodents, marsupials, etc.
    ISBN 0-87044-890-0 (regular edition)—ISBN 0-87044-968-0 (library edition)
    1. Mammals—Juvenile literature.   [1. Mammals.]   I. Title.   II. Series.
  QL706.2.B75   1993
  599—dc20
                                              93-1▮